WELCOME TO THE WORLD OF ANIMALS

Otters

Diane Swanson

Gareth Stevens Publishing
MILWAUKEE

For a free color catalog describing Gareth Stevens' list of high-quality books and multimedia programs, call 1-800-542-2595 (USA) or 1-800-461-9120 (Canada).
Gareth Stevens Publishing's Fax: (414) 225-0377.
See our catalog, too, on the World Wide Web: http://gsinc.com

The publishers acknowledge the support of the Canada Council for the Arts and the Cultural Services Branch of the Government of British Columbia in making this publication possible.

Library of Congress Cataloging-in-Publication Data

Swanson, Diane, 1944-
    [Welcome to the world of otters]
    Otters / by Diane Swanson.
        p. cm. — (Welcome to the world of animals)
    Originally published: Welcome to the world of otters. North Vancouver, B.C.:
Whitecap Books, © 1997.
    Includes index.
    Summary: Describes the physical characteristics, behavior, and habitat of both
sea otters and river otters.
    ISBN 0-8368-2214-5 (lib. bdg.)
    1. Otters—Juvenile literature. [1. Otters.] I. Title. II. Series: Swanson, Diane,
1944- Welcome to the world of animals.
QL737.C25S78   1998
599.769—dc21   98-6650

This North American edition first published in 1998 by
Gareth Stevens Publishing
1555 North RiverCenter Drive, Suite 201
Milwaukee, WI 53212 USA

This U.S. edition © 1998 by Gareth Stevens, Inc. Original edition © 1997 by Diane Swanson. First published in 1997 by Whitecap Books, Vancouver/Toronto. Additional end matter © 1998 by Gareth Stevens.

Gareth Stevens series editor: Dorothy L. Gibbs
Editorial assistant: Diane Laska
Cover design: Renee M. Bach

Cover photograph: Thomas Kitchin/First Light
Photo credits: Glen and Rebecca Grambo/First Light 4; Robert Lankinen/First Light 6, 18, 24, 30; R. A. Clevenger/WL/First Light 8; Tim Christie 10, 22; Thomas Kitchin/First Light 12, 28; Jeff Foott 14; Weimann/First Light 16; Lynn H. Stone 20; Sanford/Agliolo/First Light 26.

Printed in Mexico

1 2 3 4 5 6 7 8 9 02 01 00 99 98

Contents

World of Difference

Otters are oodles of energy bundled in fur. Although they swim and hunt for food each day, they have plenty of pep left for play.

North America has two kinds of otters: river otters and sea otters. River otters weigh up to 30 pounds (14 kilograms). Sea otters weigh two to three times more than river otters. Many sea otters are as big as large dogs.

Even the heaviest otters do not have much fat to protect them from the cold water. So, both river and sea otters have thick coats of brownish-colored fur to keep them warm.

Eating well, these sea otters might live about eight years. River otters might live more than twelve years.

This river otter's stiff whiskers sense movement, helping the otter find prey underwater.

To help them swim, otters have short legs and webbed feet. The sea otter's back feet are so long they look like floppy flippers. Special tails help make otters strong swimmers. The sea otter's wide, flat tail, however, looks nothing like the river otter's thick, ropelike tail. Special flaps of skin also help river and sea otters underwater by keeping their ears dry.

Young otters are called pups. Until it is a few months old, a river otter pup lives only with its mother. Then its father joins the family, and the otters travel and hunt together for about a year.

A sea otter pup lives only with its mother — never with its father. Mother and pup get together with other moms and pups, often forming groups of up to thirty otters. When sea otter pups are about eight months old — almost fully grown — they usually go off on their own.

FABULOUS FUR

Plunk a penny on a sea otter, and it covers about 250,000 hairs. You have less than half that many hairs on your whole head. Sea otter fur is the thickest fur in the world. It is so thick you cannot push your fingers through it.

This thick fur can hold lots of tiny air bubbles, which is how it keeps sea otters warm in cold water and helps them float. If the fur gets dirty, however, it cannot do its job. So sea otters clean themselves very often.

Where in the World

An otter in water is always right at home. Sea otters spend their lives in the sea, although close to shore. Now and then, they clamber out onto rocks, but they are awkward on land. Many never leave the water at all. Sea otters even sleep in the water. They float on their backs, often anchored in tall seaweed called kelp. Two or more sea otters will sometimes hold paws while they sleep.

River otters spend a lot of time in rivers and lakes and in water along seashores. Although they are more graceful in water, they move well — and fast — on land.

Sleepy sea otters often wrap themselves in kelp to keep from drifting away.

9

**A sunny rock makes
a great place for this
river otter to rest.**

Over short distances, they can even outrun people. River otters always sleep on land — usually wrapped around each other — in dens, under rocks, beneath tree roots, or inside hollow logs.

In water and on land, river otters are great travelers. They cover about 60 miles (97 kilometers) of waterways each year.

In winter, they often travel between waterways by sliding on ice and snow. Sometimes they tunnel through deep snow to stay out of sight.

River otters once lived all over North America. Today, they live mainly in Canada and Alaska, mostly along the Pacific coast. Different kinds of river otters live on most of the other continents.

Sea otters once lived all around the northern Pacific Ocean. Today, there are not as many sea otters as there used to be, and most of them live along the Pacific coast of North America.

OTTERS UP CLOSE

People living or working near water might see river otters snooping around docks, scrambling over boats, or searching through warehouses. Some river otters even visit peoples' houses, poking around porches and peeking into windows.

One family living on an island loved to watch river otters slide down a muddy hill near their house. They built a special little house for the otters, but the otters preferred to nest under the kitchen of the family's house.

World Full of Food

Otters need a lot of food. Food is fuel that keeps them warm and active. Each day, a sea otter eats one-fourth of its own weight in food. It munches on seaweed, but mostly it eats small sea animals, such as crabs, clams, and red sea urchins. Sea otters sometimes eat so many red sea urchins that their teeth and bones turn pink.

A sea otter dives for its dinner and snatches food with its front paws. Sometimes it tucks some of the food into "pouches" of skin under its arms, grabs a small rock, and swims to the surface. The otter can crack crab shells with its

A river otter hunts both during the day and at night. It chews its food, such as this trout, very well.

13

This sea otter is chowing down on a tasty crab.

teeth, but it needs the rock to break open clams and sea urchins. Floating on its back with the rock on its chest, it holds a clam in its front paws and smashes it onto the rock.

All through dinner, a sea otter cleans itself by rolling over in the water to wash away food scraps. After dinner, it scrubs itself thoroughly.

A river otter often eats berries and roots, but mostly it hunts animals for food. It digs in muddy river bottoms with its nose and front feet to find crayfish, salamanders, and frogs. It dives into the water — without a splash — to swim after fish. Sometimes it breaks beaver dams and grabs fish — and even young beavers — as the water level drops. In winter, river otters hunt beneath the ice that forms over the water.

A river otter feasts several times a day, gobbling up small snacks right in the water but dining out for bigger meals.

THE BEAVER'S ESCAPE

When a young beaver saw two river otters swimming its way, it dove into the water and hid under an old log on the bottom of the river.

The otters sniffed the riverbank where the beaver had been, then swam back and forth hunting for it. When the otters swam away from the beaver, it came up among the reeds to breathe. When the otters swam toward the beaver, it sank back into the water. Finally, the otters gave up the hunt, and the beaver escaped.

World of Words

When something needs to be said, an otter has to say it — and usually does! A river otter snorts to warn other otters of danger. It hums to say, "I'm mad," humming louder and higher the madder it gets. When it gets very angry — or very scared — the otter hisses. Sometimes it even SCREAMS!

When a river otter feels comfortable, it grunts like a pig or chuckles softly with other otters. It can also chirp like a bird. It chirps to make long-distance calls to other otters. On land or in the water, otters like to stay in touch.

River otters "talk" to each other by grunting and chuckling.

17

A river otter uses its keen sense of smell to find out who else has been around.

A sea otter screams wildly when something threatens it. If the otter gets cornered, it snarls and barks like a dog to say, "Go away. Now!"

When a mother sea otter dives for dinner, her pup usually has something to say about it. Left floating alone, the pup whines and makes high-pitched, screaming cries that are so loud they can be heard very far away.

"Come back. I'm hungry and frightened," it squeals.

A sea otter pup has to be loud, or its mother will not be able to hear its cries over the crashing of the ocean's waves. A mother sea otter usually responds to her pup right away. When she comes back, she cradles the pup high on her chest and coos softly to soothe it.

A mother otter's coos turn to grunts when she starts eating, but the contented sounds of her feeding soothe the pup, too.

NEWS WORTH SMELLING

River otters leave "smell-o-grams" for each other. They twist together clumps of grass with their front paws and sprinkle the grass with a strong-smelling liquid from glands in their back ends. They sprinkle this liquid also on bushes, stones, and clumps of dirt.

An otter's smell-o-gram says, "This territory is mine." A passing otter that sniffs the message might leave a smell-o-gram of its own — especially if it is looking for a mate.

New World

Otter pups are born wearing their fur coats. Sea otter pups even have their eyes open. They are perky little pups, usually born in watery beds of kelp — one pup to a mom.

Although it lives in the water, a sea otter pup cannot swim right away. So it rides on its mother's chest, snuggling, sleeping, stretching, and feeding, while she floats on her back.

The pup's mother cleans and dries it, again and again, cooing all the while. When eagles, killer whales, or people threaten her newborn, she grabs the pup with her front paws and dives underwater.

Sea otter pups, like this one, are usually born in winter. River otters are usually born in spring.

21

After leaving its den through an underwater doorway, this otter has climbed onto a rocky riverbank to shake itself dry.

River otters are born on land, often in underground dens dug by other animals. Otters are not good diggers. Most otter dens have openings to let in fresh air — and the otters.

Many dens also have underwater openings in the banks of streams or lakes. A tunnel leads from the underwater entrance to a dry nesting room inside the den. River otter pups are born in this room on a blanket of leaves, grass, and moss. Often, two or three pups are born at the same time.

Unlike sea otter pups, newborn river otters do not have their eyes open. In fact, they are not able to see for several weeks. These pups stay inside the den with their mother. She feeds and cleans them and keeps them safe at home for about three months. She also fights off any animal that tries to enter the den — even the pups' father.

FUSSY MAKES FLUFFY

A sea otter mom is very fussy. She must clean and dry her pup as soon as it is born or it will not survive the cold seawater.

As she floats on her back, the mother otter uses her front paws to roll her pup over and over on her chest. She cleans it by licking and chewing its fur. Then she blows on it to help the fur dry. She works, without stopping, for nearly two hours. When the fur is fluffy, so the pup can stay warm, the mother otter can rest for a while.

Small World

Young otters have a lot to learn. They take lessons in swimming, diving, fishing, and hunting. River otter pups start learning as soon as they leave their dens. They are usually afraid of water, at first, so a mother otter often lets her pups hold onto her as she swims. Sometimes, however, she forces them to swim by tossing them into the water or diving with them on her back.

After a few days, the pups are good swimmers — on their backs, tummies, or sides. When their father joins them, the whole family swims together. They swim in a line, one behind the other, dipping and

River otters spend their first winter with their families — and discover snow.

Three sea otters cuddle in the kelp. One of them is sniffing the air for danger, but sea otters also have good sight.

rising in the water. Some people have mistaken a swimming otter family for a long, snakelike monster.

Both parents teach a river otter pup to find its dinner. They show it how to nose out food from muddy river bottoms. They train it to charge after a fish and trap it among the rocks. All the while, they protect the pup from attacks by eagles, coyotes, and even big fish.

Sea otter pups start their lessons when they are about four weeks old. A sea otter mother leaves her pup floating while she hunts for food. At first, the pup just peeks underwater, to watch its mother dive and swim. Then it tries, harder and harder, to follow her.

Soon, the pup can dive and swim, too, and off it goes, exploring with its mom. It learns how to find food and practices cracking open clams and sea urchins with rocks.

YOUNG AND WILD

One sea otter is lively. Two are trouble. Three or more? Look out! Young sea otters are so full of energy they cannot stay still. They climb all over each other, their mothers, and sometimes even human divers.

Sea otter pups push and pull other otters and nibble their tails. They feel, sniff, and lick every shell they find. Even after hours of exploring, they do not seem tired. They just keep going, and going, and going …

Fun World

Otters have fun just being otters. It is so easy for them to find food that they have plenty of time left to play.

Just like human children, river otters like to go sliding. They slide on snow or mud, and they slide down riverbanks on their tummies, splashing into the water at the bottom.

River otters play hide-and-seek, too. While one otter dives into the snow and tunnels underneath, another one pokes its nose here and there in the snow looking for the first otter. Sometimes the otter that is hiding pokes its head out, squeals, and

Sea otters play so many games in the water. This one seems to be saying, "What will I do next?"

This river otter is looking for its playmate. Otters spot moving animals easily.

hides again. If it is caught, the two otters usually play-fight.

River otters also play with toys. They juggle sticks or pebbles with their front paws or balance these toys on their noses. Sometimes a river otter will hide a fish in the grass, just as if it were hiding a toy. Another otter will use its super sense of smell to sniff out the fish. Then, it hides the fish for the next otter.

Sea otters have toys, too. They push or climb on pieces of floating wood and use their front paws to toss and catch seaweed and shells.

Sea otter pups tumble and roll with each other or with their mothers. Sometimes they jump right out of the water together. As they play, the otters often nibble each other's ears and feet.

Playing helps keep both river and sea otters strong, healthy, and ready to hunt, but it is also just plain fun.

AWESOME OTTERS

Otters often surprise people. Here are some reasons why:

- A sea otter can dive 300 feet (91 meters) underwater.

- A river otter can stand on its two back legs, using its tail to prop itself up.

- A sea otter turns somersaults in the water to flush dirt out of its fur.

- A wet river otter rolls in powdery snow to dry so it will not freeze.

Glossary

anchor — (v) to hold firmly in place, especially in water, by attaching to something that is heavy or solid.

clamber — to climb awkwardly or with difficulty, using both hands and feet.

corner — (v) to force into a position that is uncomfortable or threatening and seems to have no easy way out.

dining — eating a main meal.

flap — a wide, flat piece of material that hangs loosely over an opening to cover it.

flush — to wash with a sudden, strong flow of water.

fuel — material consumed, such as by burning or eating, to produce some form of energy.

gland — a part of the body that produces fluid from materials in the bloodstream. The body either uses the fluid or eliminates it as waste.

kelp — a kind of seaweed that is large and brown.

plunk — to put down or drop heavily and suddenly.

Index